*Ask Me*

# CAMBRIDGE

A QUIZ

Compiled by Julia Skinner

## THE FRANCIS FRITH COLLECTION

www.francisfrith.com

First published in the United Kingdom in 2012 by The Francis Frith Collection®

This edition published exclusively for Identity Books in 2012 ISBN 978-1-84589-681-2

Text and Design copyright The Francis Frith Collection®
Photographs copyright The Francis Frith Collection® except where indicated.

The Frith® photographs and the Frith® logo are reproduced under licence from
Heritage Photographic Resources Ltd, the owners of the Frith® archive and trademarks.
'The Francis Frith Collection', 'Francis Frith' and 'Frith' are registered trademarks of
Heritage Photographic Resources Ltd.

All rights reserved. No photograph in this publication may be sold to a third party other than in the original
form of this publication, or framed for sale to a third party. No parts of this publication may be reproduced,
stored in a retrieval system, or transmitted, in any form, or by any means, electronic, mechanical, photocopying,
recording or otherwise, without the prior permission of the publishers and copyright holder.

British Library Cataloguing in Publication Data

Ask Me Another! Cambridgeshire - A Quiz
Compiled by Julia Skinner

The Francis Frith Collection
Oakley Business Park,
Wylye Road, Dinton,
Wiltshire SP3 5EU
Tel: +44 (0) 1722 716 376
Email: info@francisfrith.co.uk
www.francisfrith.com

Printed and bound in Malaysia
Contains material sourced from responsibly managed forests

Front Cover: **HARTFORD, THE RIVER AND ANCHOR INN 1907** 58555p
Frontispiece: **PETERBOROUGH, LONG CAUSEWAY 1904** 51548

*The colour-tinting is for illustrative purposes only, and is not intended to be historically accurate*

AS WITH ANY HISTORICAL DATABASE, THE FRANCIS FRITH ARCHIVE IS CONSTANTLY BEING
CORRECTED AND IMPROVED, AND THE PUBLISHERS WOULD WELCOME INFORMATION ON
OMISSIONS OR INACCURACIES

# CONTENTS

## QUESTIONS

2 Cambridgeshire Dialect Words
4 Sport
6 Arts and Literature
8 Folklore and Customs
9 History and Archaeology
16 Trade and Industry
18 General Knowledge – Cambridgeshire
26 Famous People

## ANSWERS

28 Cambridgeshire Dialect Words
30 Sport
32 Arts and Literature
34 Folklore and Customs
37 History and Archaeology
46 Trade and Industry
48 General Knowledge – Cambridgeshire
52 Famous People
54 Francis Frith - Pioneer Victorian Photographer

# Ask Me Another!
## CAMBRIDGESHIRE
### A QUIZ

# QUESTIONS

## CAMBRIDGESHIRE DIALECT WORDS

1. What were 'Fen Slodgers'?

2. What does the word 'dockey' refer to?

3. What is a 'maul'?

4. What is 'mizzle'?

5. What does it mean if someone is 'ockered'?

6. What would you keep in a 'pancheon'?

7. What would a 'scratch' be used for?

8. What would you use the word 'slubby' to describe?

9. In past times in the old county of Huntingdonshire, why would a mother be pleased rather than offended if you described her daughter as a 'strumpet'?

*Ask Me Another!*
# CAMBRIDGESHIRE
A QUIZ

**BURWELL, THE VILLAGE FROM THE CHURCH TOWER c1955**
B728007

3

# Ask Me Another!
## CAMBRIDGESHIRE
### A QUIZ

# SPORT

10. What sort of sport in Cambridgeshire involves races known as 'Bumps'?

11. What place in sporting history is held by Cambridge-born Sir John Berry 'Jack' Hobbs?

12. World championship contests of which sport took place on the frozen waterways of the Fens in the winter in Victorian times?

13. The Oxford-Cambridge Boat Race is rowed over a course of what distance?

14. The Great Court of Trinity College in Cambridge is shown in photograph 66872a (opposite). It is the largest university quadrangle in Europe, and there is a tradition linked with it known as the Great Court Run – what does this involve, and in which major film did the event feature?

15. Huntingdon Racecourse is the venue of a most unusual annual event, but it is not run by horses – what is it?

*Ask Me Another!*
# CAMBRIDGESHIRE
A QUIZ

**CAMBRIDGE, TRINITY COLLEGE, THE GREAT COURT
1914** 66872a

# Ask Me Another! CAMBRIDGESHIRE
A QUIZ

# ARTS AND LITERATURE

16. Born in what is now the Cambridgeshire village of Helpston, near Peterborough, in 1793, the son of a rustic labourer, he grew up to become celebrated for his sensitive poems describing the beauty of the countryside. He became famous in his time as 'the Peasant Poet' – who was he?

17. The breathtaking Perpendicular splendour of the medieval King's College Chapel at Cambridge is shown in the centre of photograph 60819, opposite. Amongst the treasures of the chapel are the largest and most complete set of ancient windows in the world, and a famous masterpiece by the Flemish artist Peter Paul Rubens (1577-1640) – what is it?

18. A well-known poem written about a Cambridgeshire village famously ends with the words:

    *'Stands the church clock at ten to three*
    *And is there honey still for tea?'*

    Which village was the poem about, and who was the poet?

19. What is the link between Wisbech and the novel 'Great Expectations' by Charles Dickens?

*Ask Me Another!*
# CAMBRIDGESHIRE
A QUIZ

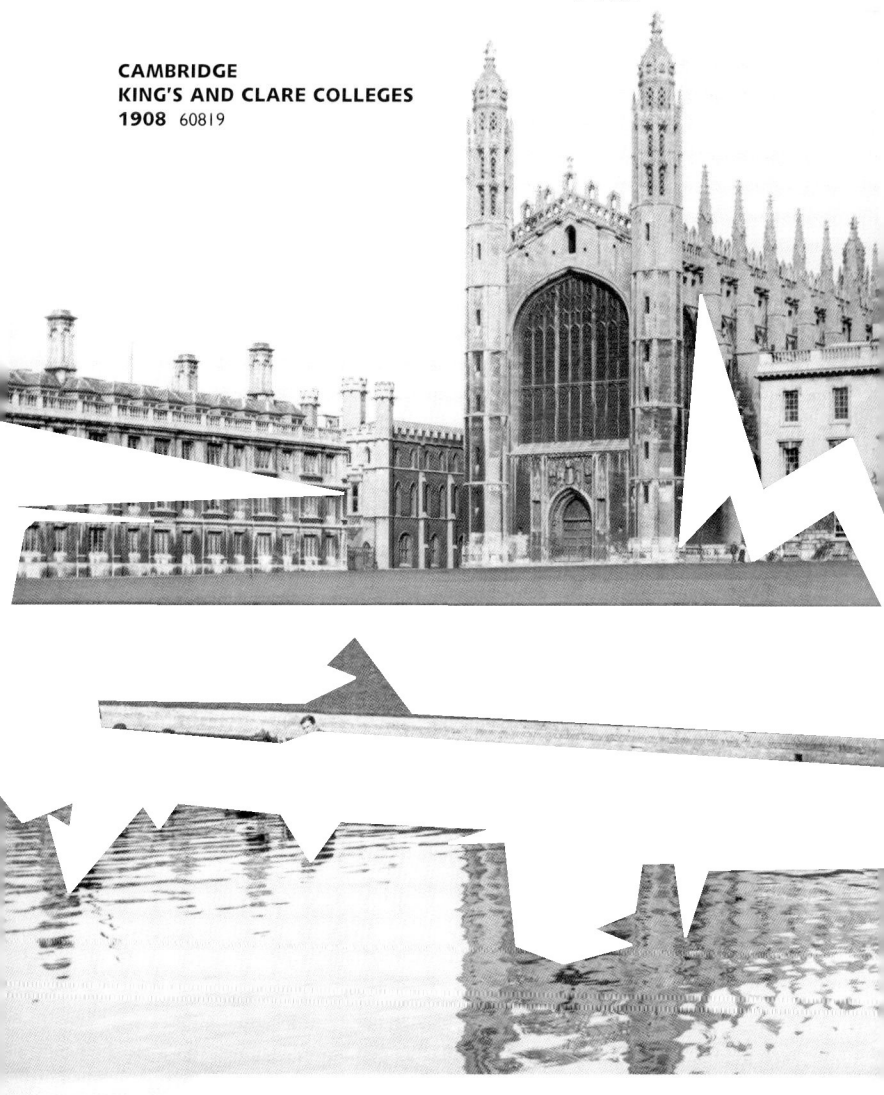

**CAMBRIDGE
KING'S AND CLARE COLLEGES
1908** 60819

# Ask Me Another!
## CAMBRIDGESHIRE
### A QUIZ

# FOLKLORE AND CUSTOMS

20. Why might some people in Cambridgeshire have carried the forefeet of a mole around in their pockets in the past?

21. In some Cambridgeshire villages in the past, why might a young couple about to get married be given a number of lumps of clay?

22. What disaster does legend say followed the lighting of an oven in Peterborough in 1116?

**BUCKDEN, HIGH STREET 1906** 55427

*Ask Me Another!*
# CAMBRIDGESHIRE
A QUIZ

# HISTORY AND ARCHAEOLOGY

23. Near Peterborough is Flag Fen, an important archaeological site from which historical period?

24. Which two queens are commemorated in the name of Queens' College in Cambridge?

25. Longthorpe Tower, about 2 miles west of Peterborough, off the A47, is a three-storey building which dates from about 1310, when the tower was added to a manor house. It contains the best-surviving example in northern Europe of … what?

26. Earith is where the two great drainage cuts of Fenland, the Old and New Bedford Rivers, take off from the Great Ouse. The drains run north-east, roughly parallel for approximately 20 miles. During the winter the strip of land known as the Ouse Washes in between the drains is allowed to flood, and is consequently a major haven for wildlife. It was in Victorian times on the Old Bedford River near Earith that a most bizarre experiment took place – what was it?

27. Which student kept a pet bear with him during his time at university in Cambridge?

28. What place in history is held by John Bellingham, probably St Neots' most infamous son?

29. Why would you have had to pay up in 1895 if you lived in Peterborough and your name was Catherine?

30. Who were the 'Adventurers', and why were they important in Cambridgeshire's history?

31. Ely Cathedral is one of the most stirring sights in Fenland; it is the fourth longest cathedral in England and has a unique eight-sided central tower. An Anglo-Saxon princess called Etheldreda (later canonised as St Etheldreda) founded the first religious community here, for women, in AD673, which was destroyed by marauding Danes in AD870; it was later re-founded as a religious house for men, following the rule of St Benedict. St Etheldreda gave a new word to the English language – what was it?

32. Which creatures were once so common in the Fens that they became a form of currency known as 'booklets' or 'sticks'?

33. How did Peterborough get its name?

**PETERBOROUGH, LONG CAUSEWAY**
**1904** 51548

**ELY, THE CATHEDRAL 1898** 40869

*Ask Me Another!*
# CAMBRIDGESHIRE
A QUIZ

## Ask Me Another!
# CAMBRIDGESHIRE
### A QUIZ

**CAMBRIDGE
QUEENS' COLLEGE
1911** 63622

*Ask Me Another!*
# CAMBRIDGESHIRE
A QUIZ

34. What is the meaning of the street name of 'Cumbergate' in Peterborough?

35. Why is there an image of a witch on a broomstick on top of the weathervane on the Jubilee Clock Tower in the square at the village of Warboys, near Huntingdon?

36. A sundial can be seen on the wall in photograph 63622 (opposite) of the Old Court of Queens' College in Cambridge. It is one of the finest examples of sundial art in the country, but is particularly noteworthy because it is also a very rare example of …what?

37. Which Anglo-Saxon freedom fighter against the Norman invaders of England attacked and burnt Peterborough to the ground in the 11th century?

38. There was once a prisoner of war camp at Norman Cross, near Stilton – prisoners from which war were held here?

39. Stilton is a small village south of Peterborough which has given its name to a famous variety of cheese – but Stilton cheese has never been made here, so how did the cheese get its name?

# Ask Me Another!
# CAMBRIDGESHIRE
## A QUIZ

**HUNTINGDON, THE OLD BRIDGE 1929** 81872

40. The River Great Ouse through Huntingdon was one of the town's greatest assets as a main route for trading; it remained a significant commercial route until the introduction of the railways in the 19th century, as well as providing the water and power necessary to produce paper in later centuries. The town also benefited from the stage-coaching traffic travelling along the Old North Road, which crosses the Great Ouse over the medieval stone bridge at Huntingdon, seen in photograph 81872, above. There is something odd about the bridge – what is it?

*Ask Me Another!*
# CAMBRIDGESHIRE
A QUIZ

41. Which three Cambridgeshire towns were known in the past as the 'Sister Towns' of the old county of Huntingdonshire?

42. How did the town of St Neots get its name?

43. A famous 17th-century civil servant and writer is said to have visited the White Horse Inn at Eaton Socon near St Neots and complained about the plainness of the maids! Who was he?

**ST NEOTS, NEW STREET 1925** 77205

# CAMBRIDGESHIRE
## A QUIZ

# TRADE AND INDUSTRY

44. Who founded an engineering company in Peterborough which used a distinctive four-circle logo on its products, and what was his company famous for making?

45. One of Cambridgeshire's towns has a long tradition as a sea port, although it is actually 10 miles inland from the sea – where is it?

46. The area around Peterborough was once an important centre for the making of which building material?

47. Several Cambridgeshire towns have a paper-making industrial heritage, but which of the county's paper towns has been called 'the cradle of the paper-making industry'?

**ELY, VIEW FROM THE WEST TOWER OF THE CATHEDRAL c1955** E34066

## Ask Me Another!
## CAMBRIDGESHIRE
A QUIZ

# GENERAL KNOWLEDGE – CAMBRIDGESHIRE

48. The modern county of Cambridgeshire has an involved and complicated history, being an amalgamation of several counties and administrative areas – can you outline all the developments since the 1950s that have made it the county it is today?

49. Which town is often called 'the Capital of the Fens'?

50. Photograph 41279 (below) shows the town centre of St Ives as it looked in 1898 – which present-day local landmark is missing from this view?

**ST IVES, MARKET SQUARE 1898**  41279

## Ask Me Another!
# CAMBRIDGESHIRE
## A QUIZ

**CAMBRIDGE, THE CAM 1914** 66902a

51. Cambridge became a city in 1951, but what was unusual about this event?

52. What is the link between Cambridge and Big Ben, the nickname for the great bell of the clock at the north-eastern end of the Palace of Westminster in London?

53. Cambridge is named after the River Cam which flows through the city and the bridge which crosses it, but what is the alternative – and original – name for the river?

54. How did a Cambridgeshire man come to give us the term 'Hobson's Choice', meaning 'no real choice at all'?

19

# Ask Me Another!
# CAMBRIDGESHIRE
## A QUIZ

55. The High Street in Kimbolton (seen in photograph K157001, below) was the market place for the surrounding villages and the site of the 'Staty' Fair that is still held every September. What was the original purpose of the 'Staty' Fair?

56. A species of tree is named after the town of Huntingdon – what is it?

**KIMBOLTON, HIGH STREET c1955** K157001

*Ask Me Another!*
# CAMBRIDGESHIRE
A QUIZ

**CAMBRIDGE, KING'S PARADE 1911** 63639

57. What are the origins of Cambridge as a university town?

58. How did Portugal Place in Cambridge get its name?

59. Where in Cambridge can you see a Man Loaded with Mischief?

# Ask Me Another!
# CAMBRIDGESHIRE
## A QUIZ

**CAMBRIDGE, THE MATHEMATICAL BRIDGE c1955** C14080

**HUNTINGDON, ALL SAINTS CHURCH AND THE WAR MEMORIAL c1955** H136014

**CAMBRIDGE THE CHURCH OF THE HOLY SEPULCHRE 1890** 26524

*Ask Me Another!*
# CAMBRIDGESHIRE
A QUIZ

60. Photograph C14080 (opposite top) shows the curious Mathematical Bridge across the River Cam at Cambridge. Why is it so called?

61. What is the connection between Huntingdon's war memorial on Market Hill and Captain Scott, the Antarctic explorer of the early 20th century? (See photograph H136014, opposite bottom.)

62. Photograph 26524 (above) shows the Church of the Holy Sepulchre in Cambridge – what is unusual about this building?

23

# Ask Me Another!
# CAMBRIDGESHIRE
## A QUIZ

**SUTTON, THE VILLAGE AND THE CHURCH c1955**  S674001

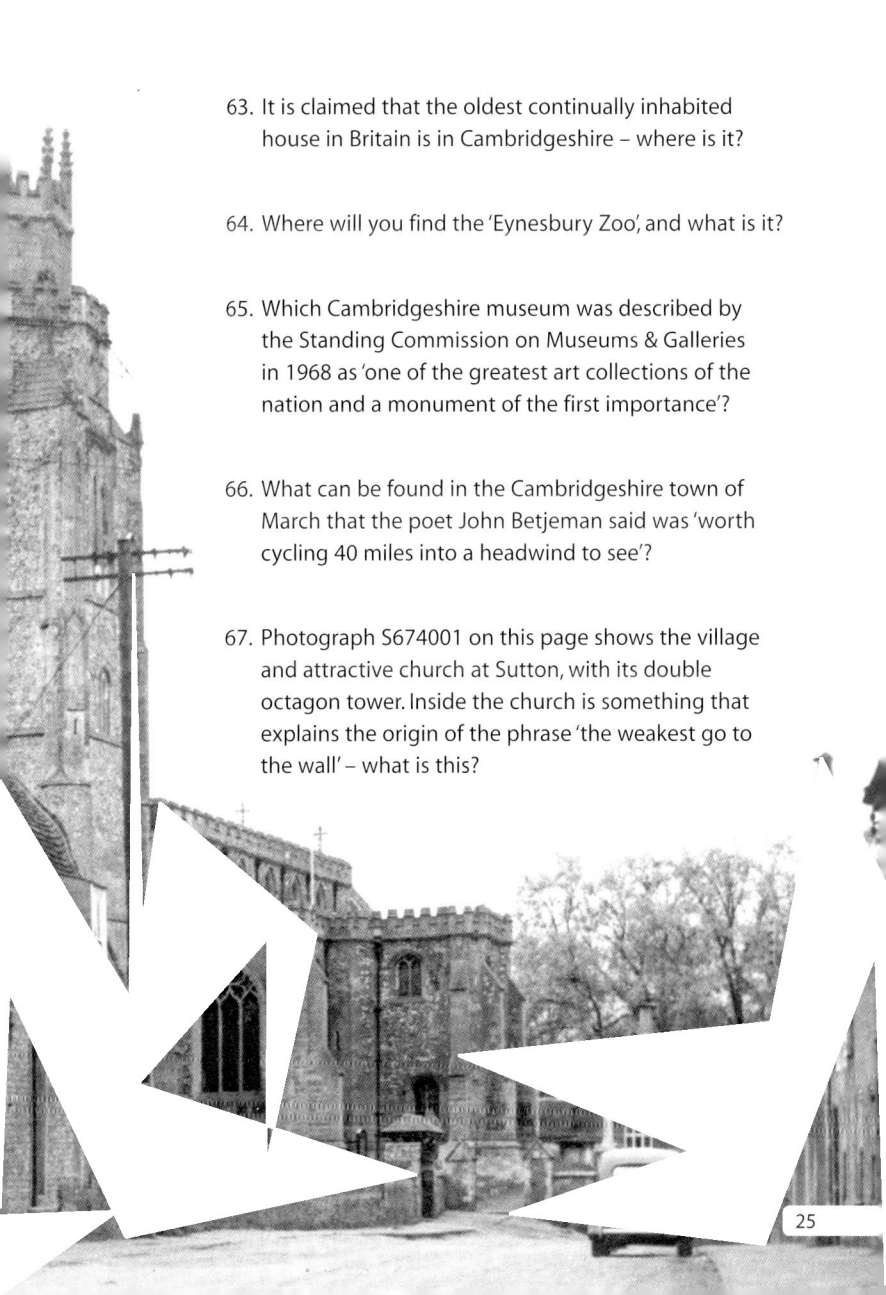

63. It is claimed that the oldest continually inhabited house in Britain is in Cambridgeshire – where is it?

64. Where will you find the 'Eynesbury Zoo', and what is it?

65. Which Cambridgeshire museum was described by the Standing Commission on Museums & Galleries in 1968 as 'one of the greatest art collections of the nation and a monument of the first importance'?

66. What can be found in the Cambridgeshire town of March that the poet John Betjeman said was 'worth cycling 40 miles into a headwind to see'?

67. Photograph S674001 on this page shows the village and attractive church at Sutton, with its double octagon tower. Inside the church is something that explains the origin of the phrase 'the weakest go to the wall' – what is this?

25

# FAMOUS PEOPLE

68. One of Wisbech's most notable landmarks is the Clarkson Memorial designed by Sir George Gilbert Scott, which is seen in photograph 47583, opposite. Who does it commemorate, and why?

69. The village green at Hilton, near Huntingdon, was landscaped by a famous landscape garden designer. Who was he, and what was the origin of the nickname by which he is usually known?

70. What is the link between Wisbech and the founding of the National Trust?

71. Which Cambridgeshire man was known in the 19th century as 'the Eynesbury Giant'?

72. Which historical figure was known by the nickname of 'Old Noll', and what was his connection with Huntingdon?

*Ask Me Another!*
# CAMBRIDGESHIRE
A QUIZ

**WISBECH**
**THE CLARKSON MEMORIAL**
**1901** 47583

# ANSWERS

## CAMBRIDGESHIRE DIALECT WORDS

1. 'Fen Slodgers' was the name given to the people who lived in the Fenland area of Cambridgeshire past, who made their living catching fish, eels and wildfowl in the wetlands and marshes of this area before the Fens were drained, and collecting reed for use as thatching material. They often moved through the water or marshes on stilts, or used vaulting poles to move around where the water was deep. 'Fen Slodger' communities lived on embanked areas of land in the Fens where they had created islands where they could raise crops and keep livestock.

2. 'Dockey' is the name for the mid-day snack at work. The most usual interpretation for this is that it gets its name from when wages were 'docked' for the time that workers took off for their meal break. However, the word 'dockey' may actually come from the time when farmers 'docked' their ploughs whilst they took their elevenses.

3. A 'maul' is a mallet.

4. 'Mizzle' is mist.

5. If someone is being 'ockered', they are being awkward or contrary.

6. A 'pancheon' is a container for keeping bread in, ie a bread bin.

*Ask Me Another!*
# CAMBRIDGESHIRE
A QUIZ

**HARTFORD, THE RIVER AND ANCHOR INN 1907** 58555

7. A 'scratch' was the name for a bench used for dressing slaughtered pigs.

8. 'Slubby' describes squelchy, runny mud.

9. In the former county of Huntingdonshire, now part of Cambridgeshire, the word 'strumpet' was used in the past to describe a healthy, hearty child. Nowadays it has a more uncomplimentary meaning!

# Ask Me Another!
## CAMBRIDGESHIRE
### A QUIZ
# SPORT

10. Cambridge has a long history of rowing, as both a leisure and a sporting activity. Because the River Cam is not wide enough for conventional races, races called 'Bumps' are held. Eights such as the one seen in photograph 61516 (below) start off some 1½ lengths behind one another, and each boat has to catch up with the one in front, 'bumping' it.

11. Born in Cambridge in 1882, Sir John Berry 'Jack' Hobbs, the Surrey and England batsman, was the world's greatest cricket batsman of his time. Between 1905 and 1934 he played in 61 test matches and scored a record 61,237 runs. Perhaps his greatest innings at the Oval was against Australia in 1926, when he made a century to help bring back the Ashes to England. The list of his batting achievements is extensive but here are a few highlights: he scored 197 centuries in first class cricket, the most by any player in any country to date; he is the oldest man in cricketing history to have scored a test match century (at the age of 46); in 1953 he became the first professional cricketer to be knighted; and half his total of centuries were scored after the age of 40. In the year 2000, Wisden selected him as one of the top five players of the 20th century.

**CAMBRIDGE, THE EIGHTS 1909** 61516

12. There has been a long tradition of ice skating on the frozen waterways of the Fens in winter, and Mare Fen in Swavesey was held to be the best place in the whole of Fenland for skating in Victorian times – world skating championships were even held there when the conditions were right. The greatest ice skating race in Fenland history took place in 1895, when the competitors started at Bottisham Locks at Waterbeach, raced to Ely and back, and then back into Ely. Although the distance was 30 miles, the result was a dead heat!

13. The Oxford-Cambridge Boat Race is rowed over a course of 4½ miles.

14. The Great Court Run is an attempt to run round the perimeter of Great Court in the 43 seconds that the college clock takes to strike twelve o'clock. It is believed that the only two people to have actually completed the run in the required time are Lord Burghley, who did it in 1927, and Sebastian Coe, who beat Steve Cram in a charity race in October 1988. Technically, Lord Burghley was the second person to have completed the run in time, as someone had done it in the 1890s, but at that date the clock took five seconds longer to complete its toll. Lord Burghley's successful attempt inspired the race scene in the film 'Chariots of Fire', in which the character of Lord Andrew Lindsay is loosely based on Burghley, although in the film the feat is actually achieved by Harold Abrahams. The race scene in 'Chariots of Fire' was not filmed in the Great Court though, but at Eton.

15. Huntingdon Racecourse is the venue of the Mascot Grand National, an annual race over giant hurdles between the mascots of various football and other sporting teams, as well as mascots from non-sports organisations. Previous winners included 'Beau Brummie Bulldog' from Birmingham City FC (winner of the first event in 1999), 'Harry the Hornet' from Watford FC (winner in 2000), 'Caddy the Owl' from Oldham AFC (winner in both 2002 and 2003), and 'Scoop the Squirrel', the mascot of the Sun newspaper (winner in 2006).

# Ask Me Another! CAMBRIDGESHIRE
A QUIZ

# ARTS AND LITERATURE

16. John Clare. Photograph H434006 (below) shows the cottage in Helpston where he was born and grew up, the son of a farmworker. He loved the countryside and the rural way of life, and his 'Poems Descriptive of Rural Life' was published in 1820 to great acclaim. Sadly, he went insane in later life and ended his days in Northampton Asylum, but his works have remained popular. After his death he was buried in St Botolph's churchyard at Helpston. In 2005 The John Clare Trust purchased his birthplace, Clare Cottage in Helpston, preserving it for future generations. The cottage has been restored using traditional building methods, to create a centre where people can learn about John Clare, his works, and rural life in the early 19th century.

**HELPSTON, CLARE COTTAGE c1955** H434006

*Ask Me Another!*
# CAMBRIDGESHIRE
A QUIZ

**ST IVES, THE OLD RIVER 1914**  66958

17. 'The Adoration of the Magi', which is displayed behind the altar of the chapel.

18. Grantchester, a few miles from Cambridge – the lines end the poem titled 'The Old Vicarage, Grantchester' by Rupert Brooke. It is believed that the church clock was broken when the poet was living in Grantchester, with the hands stuck at 'ten to three'. For some years after Rupert Brooke's death in the First World War, the clock was kept at this time as a memorial to him.

19. The Wisbech and Fenland Museum in Wisbech contains a library of over 12,000 volumes. One collection of particular importance is the bequest of the Reverend Chauncy Hare Townshend that includes the original manuscript of 'Great Expectations' by Charles Dickens. The manuscript is on view to the public on the first Saturday of the month.

# FOLKLORE AND CUSTOMS

20. The people of the damp Fenlands were very prone to rheumatic complaints in the past. A local folklore belief was that rheumatic complaints could be prevented or alleviated by carrying the forefeet of a mole around in your pocket. Examples of these can be seen in the Cambridge and County Folk Museum on Castle Street in Cambridge.

21. Clay lump was an economical form of material for building houses in parts of Cambridgeshire in the 19th century. The clay, dug out close by and generally leaving a pond in its wake, was mixed with straw to form a thick slurry which was then either moulded in wooden frames into blocks and dried in the sun, or poured straight into shuttering to make the walls. The outside of the house was then rendered to protect it from the weather. It was a tradition in some Cambridgeshire villages for a young couple about to get married to be presented with a number of clay lumps as a start towards building their own home. For those who could afford it, the finished building would then be cased in Cambridgeshire stock brick, or disguised by a plaster render, 'lined out' to look like stone blocks.

22. In 1116 a major fire destroyed the monastery buildings and church at Peterborough. Legend says that the fire was caused when a monk, struggling to light the bake-house oven, cursed it and cried: 'Devil light the fire!'. Work on a new church began in 1118. When Henry VIII dissolved the monasteries, the monastery church at Peterborough became a cathedral, by a special dispensation of the king in 1541; his first wife, Catherine of Aragon, was buried there and he did not want the place to fall into disrepair. The building remains Peterborough's chief glory, and has one of the most famous west fronts in England, built in the Early English style (see photograph 69083, opposite); the dominant feature is the trio of huge arches with their ornate mouldings and pointed gables above. Inside, Peterborough Cathedral is one of only three churches in Europe with a surviving medieval painted wooden ceiling in its nave. Peterborough's dates from c1220, and the paintings include saints and monsters.

*Ask Me Another!*
# CAMBRIDGESHIRE
A QUIZ

**PETERBOROUGH
THE CATHEDRAL
THE WEST FRONT
1919** 69083

35

*Ask Me Another!*
# CAMBRIDGESHIRE
## A QUIZ

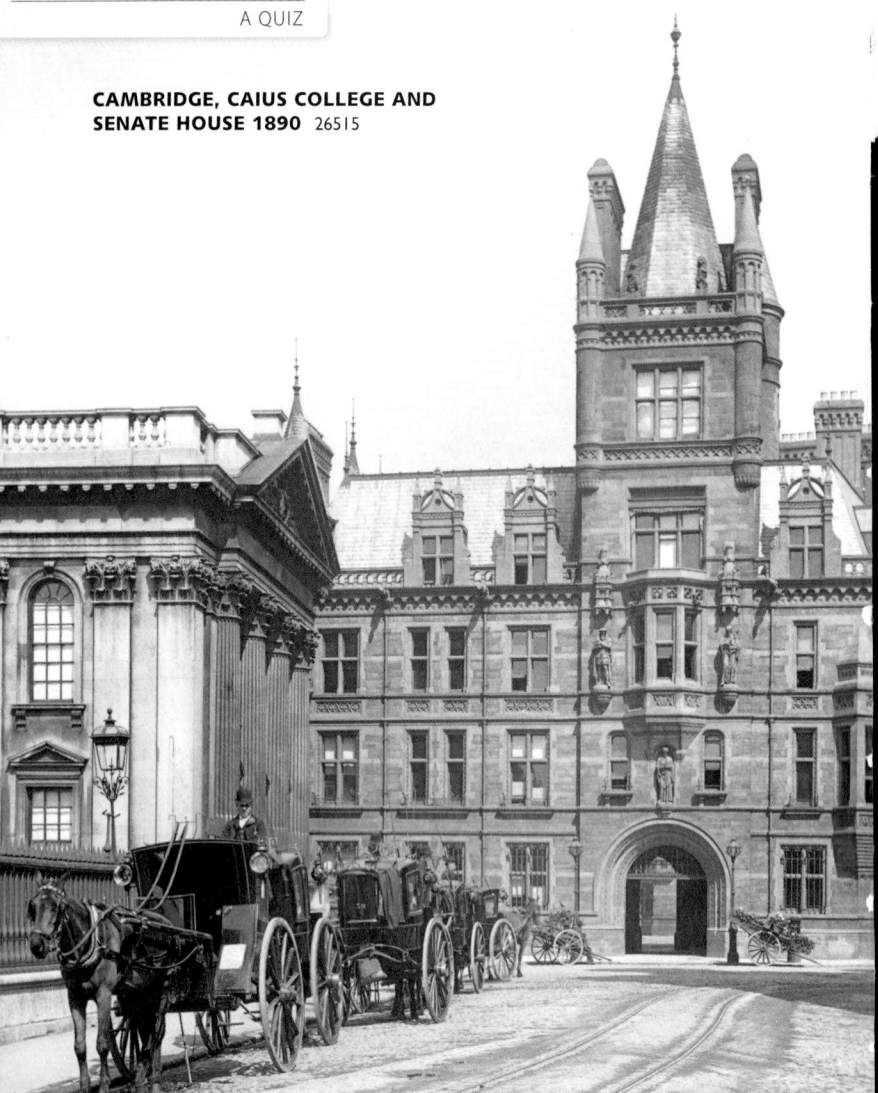

**CAMBRIDGE, CAIUS COLLEGE AND SENATE HOUSE 1890** 26515

*Ask Me Another!*
# CAMBRIDGESHIRE
A QUIZ

# HISTORY AND ARCHAEOLOGY

23. Flag Fen is a Bronze Age site that was probably used for religious purposes. A large number of poles across the wet Fenland, arranged in five very long rows (around 1km), connected Whittlesey Island with the Peterborough area. A small island was formed part way across the structure, which may have been where ritual ceremonies took place. At the visitor centre many of the artefacts that have been found can be seen, including what is believed to be the oldest wheel in Britain, as well as reconstructions of Bronze Age and Iron Age roundhouses.

24. Margaret of Anjou, wife and queen of Henry VI, who first founded the college in 1448, and Elizabeth Woodville, wife and queen of Edward IV, who re-founded the college in 1465.

25. Longthorpe Tower, in the care of English Heritage, contains the best-surviving example in northern Europe of English medieval wall paintings, dating from the 14th century. Subjects include the Wheel of Life and the Nativity.

26. A wager had been placed on whether or not the earth was flat, and the Old Bedford River was chosen as the location to prove or disprove the theory, as it was the longest, straightest stretch of calm water in the country. The experiment was performed using three boats with masts of equal height moored along the length of the river. When sighted through a telescope the masts were found not to be in line, and the Flat-Earther who had instigated the experiment was discredited.

# CAMBRIDGESHIRE
A QUIZ

27. The poet Lord Byron. Whilst he was a student at Cambridge he was annoyed that the university rules banned him from keeping a dog. With characteristic perversity, he installed a tame bear instead, arguing that there was no mention of bears in the statutes. The college authorities had no legal basis to complain, and the bear stayed until Byron graduated, when it went with the poet to his ancestral home at Newstead Abbey.

28. John Bellingham was born in St Neots in 1776. His job with a Liverpool merchant involved travelling to Russia. When contracts he negotiated there failed, he was jailed. On his return to England he applied for compensation but was refused, which made him very bitter. On 11th May 1812, Bellingham went to the House of Commons and shot and killed the Prime Minster, Spencer Perceval; he was arrested at the scene, tried with some haste and hanged.

29. Catherine of Aragon, the first wife of Henry VIII, was confined in one of the corner turrets of the Great Tower at Buckden (once the palace of the Bishops of Lincoln) and later at Kimbolton Castle following her divorce from the king, both in Cambridgeshire. She died at Kimbolton Castle in 1536, and was buried in Peterborough Cathedral. Her tomb was destroyed in 1643, but in 1895 a slab of Irish marble to commemorate her in the cathedral was provided and paid for by all the women in Peterborough named Catherine, in honour of the unhappy queen.

*Ask Me Another!*
# CAMBRIDGESHIRE
A QUIZ

**BUCKDEN
THE GREAT TOWER
c1950** B237009

/ Ask Me Another!
# CAMBRIDGESHIRE
## A QUIZ

**PETERBOROUGH, THE CATHEDRAL FROM THE INFIRMARY ARCHES 1890** 24444

30. For hundreds of years the Fens existed as wild and desolate marshland of sedge and reeds, with outcrops of land forming 'islands', such as Ely, Thorney and Ramsey. In summer it was possible to graze sheep and cattle, but in winter the rivers overflowed, flooding the peaty countryside so that no agriculture was possible. The Romans tried unsuccessfully to drain the land, but it was not until the 17th century that sufficient technology existed to tackle the reclamation of the Fens. The Earl of Bedford and other men of vision and capital employed a Dutch engineer, Cornelius Vermuyden, to drain the Fenland by constructing drainage cuts; these men were known as 'Adventurers', because they 'adventured' capital in return for allotments of the reclaimed land.

31. St Etheldreda was also known as St Audrey in the Middle Ages, and a cheap variety of bobbin lace was sold at stalls at the annual St Audrey's Fair at Ely on her feast day. In time all poor quality lace became known as 'St Audrey's', which eventually became shortened to 'tawdry', used to describe something cheap and showy, but of low value.

32. Eels were once so common in the Fens that they became a form of currency known as 'booklets' or 'sticks' of eels, with which land rent could be paid to the Church or State. One 'stick' comprised 25 eels.

33. The Anglo-Saxons established a town and a monastery called Medeshamstede at what is now Peterborough, but it was destroyed in Viking raids. St Aethelwold, Bishop of Winchester, came here to restore the monastery and built a large new religious house, enclosing it with strong walls and calling it a burgh; later, the name of the saint to whom the monastery was dedicated was added to the name of the burgh, to create Peter Burgh, which later became Peterborough.

*Ask Me Another!*
# CAMBRIDGESHIRE
A QUIZ

34. Cumbergate in Peterborough is so-named because it was the area of the medieval town where the woolcombers lived and worked. Woolcombing was part of the process of manufacturing worsted cloth, and was a highly skilled and important trade within the medieval textile industry which was so important to East Anglia in the Middle Ages.

35. Warboys was the scene of a notorious witch-hunt in Elizabethan times, when ten-year-old Jane Throckmorton, daughter of Robert Throckmorton, Squire of Warboys, accused 80-year-old Alice Samuel of bewitching her; she was experiencing fits, and complained of painful prickling sensations on her skin, like a cat scratching her. The charge was repeated by her four sisters, some household servants, and also by Lady Cromwell, grandmother of Oliver Cromwell, who was visiting the family at the time; Lady Cromwell berated Alice for causing such affliction and forcibly cut off a lock of her hair to burn, in hopes of weakening the witch's power; she subsequently fell ill and died. Alice Samuel, her husband and daughter were arrested and taken to Huntingdon in April 1593, where they were tried for the murder by witchcraft of Lady Cromwell; they were found guilty and hanged. The three purported witches are commemorated by the image of a witch on her broomstick on top of the weathervane on the Jubilee Clock Tower in the square at Warboys. In recent years a theory has been put forward that the symptoms of 'witchcraft' which the Throckmorton girls experienced (fits, hallucinations and painful skin) might have been caused by ergot poisoning – ergot is a fungus which infects rye grain, and rye was a staple crop in East Anglia at that time.

## Ask Me Another!
# CAMBRIDGESHIRE
### A QUIZ

**ST NEOTS, MILL LANE 1897** 39986

36. The sundial in the Old Court of Queens' College in Cambridge, which dates from 1642, is also one of the very few moondials in existence. The shadow cast on the golden Roman numerals tells apparent solar time, and the table of figures below the dial is an aid to telling the time by moonlight, providing the moon is strong enough to cast a reasonable shadow.

37. A famous episode in Peterborough's history is the attack on the monastery and town in 1069 by the Anglo-Saxon guerrilla fighter Hereward the Wake ('the watchful'), as part of his resistance to Norman rule. The town was burned to the ground and the church stripped of all its valuables; Hereward used the appointment of an unpopular Norman abbot, Turold, as the excuse for doing this. He took refuge in the Isle of Ely, protected by the surrounding marshes, and held out there for around three years. The Normans made several unsuccessful attempts at besieging the Isle, which included trying to lay a causeway across a narrow stretch of Fen, probably at Aldreth or Stuntney. They did break into Ely eventually, but Hereward managed to escape. Legend says that after his death he was buried in the abbey grounds at Crowland, in Lincolnshire.

38. French prisoners of war from the Napoleonic Wars of the early 19th century were kept at the prison camp at Norman Cross, near Stilton. They amused themselves by carving models from meat bones and making straw marquetry pictures, and selling them locally. There is a permanent exhibition of some of these carvings and straw pictures at the Peterborough Museum. Some of the models are automated, such as a castle with miniature soldiers, or elaborate guillotines, and are breathtaking in their intricacy. There is also a wonderful model of Peterborough Cathedral.

39. Stilton is a small village south of Peterborough with a reputation for a cheese which it has actually never produced. The village was an important staging point on the Great North Road, and Leicestershire farmers took their produce to the 17th-century Bell Inn at Stilton to be transported by coach to London; thus Stilton cheese was named after its distribution centre, rather than its place of production. Even so, each year there is a cheese-rolling charity race along the village, with local teams, many in fancy dress, bowling a 'cheese' (usually a log cut and painted to resemble a cheese) along the High Street. The winning team receives a crate of beer and a real cheese.

## CAMBRIDGESHIRE
A QUIZ

40. The medieval stone bridge over the Great Ouse at Huntingdon was constructed in 1332 to connect the town with Godmanchester on the opposite bank of the river. The respective authorities paid for three arches each, with the builders starting on each bank and meeting in the middle – and working to a different design! The pedestrian refuges built by Godmanchester are three-sided, while those built by Huntingdon are two-sided.

41. The towns of St Neots, Huntingdon and St Ives were known in the past as the 'Sister Towns' of Huntingdonshire.

42. St Neots is named after St Neot, whose bones were brought there from Cornwall to give status to the new priory that had been established here by Earl Leofric around AD975. It is not clear whether the bones were actually stolen from the Cornish village that is now called St Neot or not, but the local people there were understandably very upset at the loss of their saint's relics. In the late 11th century Richard de Clare and his wife, Rohais, had the priory buildings rebuilt on the present Priory Centre site in St Neots. Sadly, nothing of these Norman buildings remains visible today, but excavations have shown they were extensive, covering at least 50 acres. St Neots Priory was closed in 1539 during Henry VIII's dissolution of the monasteries; all its relics, including the bones of St Neot, disappeared, and no one knows what happened to them. The priory buildings were allowed to decay, and the stone was taken away and re-used elsewhere, possibly some being used on a new town bridge.

43. This was Samuel Pepys, the famous diarist who was also Secretary to the Navy. He owned property at Brampton, and was often in the area.

# Ask Me Another!
## CAMBRIDGESHIRE
### A QUIZ

# TRADE AND INDUSTRY

44. Frank Perkins. He was the son of an agricultural engineer in Peterborough, and worked for the family firm of Barford and Perkins. During the depression of the 1930s he founded his own business in the city, developing high-quality diesel engines. His four-circle badge became an internationally famous sign of excellence. In the mid 20th century small diesel Perkins engines were used to power the pumps of the Fenland drainage systems, but nowadays the water from the Cambridgeshire basin is controlled by electric pumps.

45. Wisbech. Although it is 10 miles from the sea on what is now an artificial River Nene, Wisbech has a long tradition as a sea port. Vessels brought in coal from north-east England and timber from the Baltic, and vast quantities of corn also passed through the town's markets. Large granaries were raised along Nene Quay and the west bank of the river from the bridge to West Parade; most of the buildings that survive have now been converted into flats. Even in modern times, boats laden with oranges and bananas would come up to the warehouses on the west bank at the rear of the Old Market, but with the opening of the Freedom Bridge in 1971 this became impossible. The port is not so busy now, mainly through the rise of Sutton Bridge with its better links with South Lincolnshire and Norfolk. The wealth created by years of shipping has given Wisbech two of the most perfect Georgian streets in England – the North and South Brinks, sombre rows of mansions and warehouses which look out over each other on opposite sides of the river.

*Ask Me Another!*
# CAMBRIDGESHIRE
A QUIZ

46. The area around Peterborough was an important brick-making centre in the past, supporting several companies, most of which eventually merged into the London Brick Company. Although the London Brick Company originated from Peterborough, it derived its name from supplying the capital's increasing needs for building materials.

47. St Neots. St Neots Paper Mills were established in 1804 when the mill at the end of St Neots Common was converted from corn milling by the Fourdrinier brothers. The advances in paper manufacture made by their inventions led to St Neots being called 'the cradle of the paper-making industry'. The old paper mill buildings were demolished in 2002 to make way for residential and community development.

**WISBECH, THE DOCKS AND TIMBER YARDS c1955** W115047

# Ask Me Another!
## CAMBRIDGESHIRE
A QUIZ

# GENERAL KNOWLEDGE – CAMBRIDGESHIRE

48. In the 1950s the area now known as Cambridgeshire comprised four distinct areas: two ancient counties, Huntingdonshire and Cambridgeshire, the Soke of Peterborough, and the Isle of Ely. In 1965 the Soke of Peterborough, an independent authority since 1888, was combined with Huntingdonshire. On 1 April 1974 Huntingdonshire was merged with Cambridgeshire and the Isle of Ely, the new county being known as Cambridgeshire. The city of Peterborough is now in Cambridgeshire, although at one time it was just within the north-east boundary of Northamptonshire.

49. Wisbech is often called 'the Capital of the Fens'.

50. The statue of Oliver Cromwell, shown in photograph 48069 (right), which stands in the Market Square by the Free Church and was erected in 1901. The local townsfolk raised the money for the statue by public subscription, to mark the fact that Cromwell had lived at St Ives from 1631 to 1635.

**ST IVES, THE STATUE OF OLIVER CROMWELL MARKET HILL 1901** 48069

*Ask Me Another!*
# CAMBRIDGESHIRE
A QUIZ

51. Cambridge was granted its city charter in 1951 even though it does not have a cathedral, which is usually a prerequisite for city status.

52. The clock of Great St Mary's Church, the official University church, chimes a tune which was specially written for it in 1793, and which was later copied for Big Ben in London.

53. The other, original, name for the River Cam is the River Granta. The earliest recorded reference to a bridge at Cambridge is in the Anglo-Saxon Chronicle for AD875, when the name for the settlement is Grantebrycg. By Norman times the name of the town had become Grentabrige or Cantebrigge, while the river was still called the Granta. Over time the name of the town changed to Cambridge, but the river was still known as the Granta for a considerable period, and indeed is still often referred to as the Granta to this day. The name of the river was eventually changed to the Cam to match the name of the town.

54. Thomas Hobson (1544-1631) ran a livery stable in Cambridge and inspired the phrase 'Hobson's Choice' because he refused to allow customers to choose their own horses – it was his choice, or none at all. He was later Mayor of Cambridge and paid for Hobson's Conduit, which originally stood close to what is now the Guildhall, but was moved to its current site on Lensfield Corner when the Market Square was created.

55. The 'Staty Fair' at Kimbolton was originally the hiring fair for farm labourers and domestic servants, but today it is just for fun.

56. A species of elm tree is named the Huntingdon Elm, Ulmus × hollandica 'Vegeta'. It was developed at the nursery of Wood and Ingram at Brampton, near Huntingdon, in the 1740s.

# Ask Me Another!
# CAMBRIDGESHIRE
## A QUIZ

57. In 1209 a group of scholars came to Cambridge from Oxford, after some of their number had been accused of murder and hanged in Oxford by the townspeople. Many of them returned to Oxford later, but enough remained in Cambridge to form a scholastic community. By the mid 13th century, this gathering of students and teachers was recognised as a University, despite the fact that they had no buildings of their own. In 1284, the first college was built; it was sited next to a church dedicated to St Peter, and was duly named Peterhouse by its founder, Hugh de Balsam, the Bishop of Ely. Over the next 200 years or so, more colleges were added. While monastic properties fell to Henry VIII's Reformation in the 16th century, the colleges of Cambridge remained secure; in fact the king even used the proceeds of dissolved religious establishments to set up his own college, when he merged Michaelhouse and King's Hall into Trinity College.

58. Portugal Place derives its name not from the country of Portugal, but from the port which was once shipped into Cambridge in vast quantities, brought by barges to the nearby Quayside, and taken from there to college dining tables.

59. At the Cambridge and County Folk Museum on Castle Street. 'The Man Loaded with Mischief' is on an inn sign, one of four such signs held at the museum which were painted by the local artist Richard Hopkins Leach in the 1840s.

60. The Mathematical Bridge at Cambridge is built on geometric principles and was the first bridge in the world to be designed according to a mathematical analysis of the forces within it. The bridge was originally held together – so the story goes – without any fixing devices. However, it was taken apart in 1867 to discover the principles upon which it was built, and sadly those who dismantled it were unable to reassemble it without the use of bolts.

61. 'The Thinking Soldier' war memorial on Market Hill was designed by the sculptress Kathleen Hilton Young, who before her second marriage in 1922 was Lady Kathleen Scott, the widow of the Antarctic explorer Captain Scott who died in 1912. It was erected in 1923.

62. The Church of the Holy Sepulchre in Bridge Street in Cambridge is one of only four round churches remaining in England; it was founded in 1130 by the Knights Templar on the model of the Church of the Holy Sepulchre in Jerusalem. It is usually referred to in Cambridge as the Round Church.

63. The Manor House at Hemingford Grey near St Ives was built c1130, and is said to be the oldest continually inhabited house in Britain. The writer Lucy Maria Wood Boston bought the Manor in 1939 and used it as the inspiration for her series of six children's stories known as the Green Knowe books. The house is open to the public by appointment.

64. In the church at Eynesbury, near St Neots. The church contains some medieval benches with ornate carved ends, some of which are in the shape of birds or exotic animals and are known locally as the 'Eynesbury Zoo'.

65. The Fitzwilliam Museum in Trumpington Street in Cambridge. Amongst its treasures are the most complete collection of medieval British coins in existence, and an outstanding collection of medieval illustrated manuscripts.

66. John Betjeman said that it was 'worth cycling 40 miles into a headwind to see' the church that March is famous for – the roof of St Wendreda's Church is a testament to the carpenter's art, a hammerbeam roof with 120 carved wooden angels playing musical instruments.

67. Inside the church at Sutton, a bench runs along the wall for the use of those who could not stand throughout the lengthy services of the Middle Ages. Benches like this gave rise to the saying 'the weakest go to the wall'.

51

# FAMOUS PEOPLE

68. The Clarkson Memorial in Wisbech commemorates the town's most famous son, Thomas Clarkson (1760-1846), who was a key figure in the fight to abolish the slave trade of the 18th and 19th centuries. He dedicated his life to travelling the country speaking in support of William Wilberforce's anti-slavery movement; in 1996 his efforts were given national recognition when a memorial plaque to him was placed in Westminster Abbey.

69. The village green at Hilton was landscaped by Lancelot 'Capability' Brown, who lived at the nearby Fenstanton Manor. This famous 18th-century landscape gardener was given the nickname of 'Capability' because of his habit of commenting on the 'capabilities' of the sites he was commissioned to work on. His tomb lies in the church at Fenstanton.

70. A co-founder of the National Trust was Octavia Hill (1838-1912), who was born in a house at South Brink in Wisbech. Miss Hill was also a tireless housing and social reformer and part of the fine house where she was born is now a museum dedicated to her life and work.

71. James Toller was 'the Eynesbury Giant'. He was born in 1798 and could not stop growing. When he died in 1818, aged 22, it is thought that he was just over eight feet tall. During his short life he first served in the army, then later travelled the country, appearing in public exhibitions as a giant, until ill-health forced him to return home to Eynesbury, now a suburb of St Neots. When he died he was buried at an unmarked spot inside Eynesbury church for fear of grave robbers stealing his body to sell for anatomical research. He is commemorated in the name of Toller Mews, a housing development in Eynesbury, and a plaque commemorating him has been put up in Eynesbury near the former home of the Toller family in Rectory Lane, off St Mary Street.

*Ask Me Another!*
# CAMBRIDGESHIRE
A QUIZ

72. 'Old Noll' was the nickname of Huntingdon's most famous son, Oliver Cromwell, who was born in a house in the main street of the town in 1599. He was educated at the grammar school in Huntingdon before becoming MP for Cambridge and ultimately Lord Protector of England, Scotland and Ireland after the Civil War of the 17th century. The house where he was born no longer stands in Huntingdon (the 19th-century Cromwell House was built on its site), but the old grammar school in the town which he attended still survives, and is now a museum devoted to Cromwell and the 'Great Rebellion' of 1640-1660 (see photograph 81880, opposite), containing an impressive collection and display of memorabilia relating to the Lord Protector. In the political and religious turmoil of the mid 17th century, as King Charles I and Parliament fought for power, Oliver Cromwell's strong views and forthright manner brought him to the fore very quickly, and through the bitter struggles of the Civil War he was to show himself to be the most able military leader of the Parliamentarian forces. Though he lacked military experience when the war broke out, he moulded a superb cavalry force, provided inspired leadership and rose in three years from the rank of captain to that of lieutenant-general. He was a prime mover in the trial and execution of King Charles I, after which he became Lord Protector of the Commonwealth, king in all but name. Ruthless, charismatic and devoutly religious, he was one of the most loved or hated men of his age.

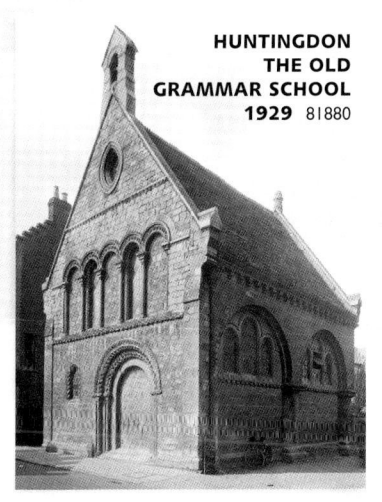

**HUNTINGDON
THE OLD
GRAMMAR SCHOOL
1929** 81880

# FRANCIS FRITH

## PIONEER VICTORIAN PHOTOGRAPHER

Francis Frith, founder of the world-famous photographic archive, was a complex and multi-talented man. A devout Quaker and a highly successful Victorian businessman, he was philosophical by nature and pioneering in outlook. By 1855 he had already established a wholesale grocery business in Liverpool, and sold it for the astonishing sum of £200,000, which is the equivalent today of over £15,000,000. Now in his thirties, and captivated by the new science of photography, Frith set out on a series of pioneering journeys up the Nile and to the Near East.

## INTRIGUE AND EXPLORATION

He was the first photographer to venture beyond the sixth cataract of the Nile. Africa was still the mysterious 'Dark Continent', and Stanley and Livingstone's historic meeting was a decade into the future. The conditions for picture taking confound belief. He laboured for hours in his wicker dark-room in the sweltering heat of the desert, while the volatile chemicals fizzed dangerously in their trays. Back in London he exhibited his photographs and was 'rapturously cheered' by members of the Royal Society. His reputation as a photographer was made overnight.

## VENTURE OF A LIFE-TIME

By the 1870s the railways had threaded their way across the country, and Bank Holidays and half-day Saturdays had been made obligatory by Act of Parliament. All of a sudden the working man and his family were able to enjoy days out, take holidays, and see a little more of the world.

With typical business acumen, Francis Frith foresaw that these new tourists would enjoy having souvenirs to commemorate their days out. For the next thirty years he travelled the country by train and by pony and trap, producing fine photographs of seaside resorts and beauty spots that were keenly bought by millions of Victorians. These prints were painstakingly pasted into family albums and pored over during the dark nights of winter, rekindling precious memories of summer excursions. Frith's studio was soon supplying retail shops all over the country, and by 1890 F Frith & Co had become the greatest specialist photographic publishing company in the world, with over 2,000 sales outlets, and pioneered the picture postcard.

## FRANCIS FRITH'S LEGACY

Francis Frith had died in 1898 at his villa in Cannes, his great project still growing. By 1970 the archive he created contained over a third of a million pictures showing 7,000 British towns and villages.

Frith's legacy to us today is of immense significance and value, for the magnificent archive of evocative photographs he created provides a unique record of change in the cities, towns and villages throughout Britain over a century and more. Frith and his fellow studio photographers revisited locations many times down the years to update their views, compiling for us an enthralling and colourful pageant of British life and character.

We are fortunate that Frith was dedicated to recording the minutiae of everyday life. For it is this sheer wealth of visual data, the painstaking chronicle of changes in dress, transport, street layouts, buildings, housing and landscape that captivates us so much today, offering us a powerful link with the past and with the lives of our ancestors.

Computers have now made it possible for Frith's many thousands of images to be accessed almost instantly. The archive offers every one of us an opportunity to examine the places where we and our families have lived and worked down the years. Its images, depicting our shared past, are now bringing pleasure and enlightenment to millions around the world a century and more after his death.

For further information visit: www.francisfrith.com

## INTERIOR DECORATION

Frith's photographs can be seen framed and as giant wall murals in thousands of pubs, restaurants, hotels, banks, retail stores and other public buildings throughout Britain. These provide interesting and attractive décor, generating strong local interest and acting as a powerful reminder of gentler days in our increasingly busy and frenetic world.

## FRITH PRODUCTS

All Frith photographs are available as prints and posters in a variety of different sizes and styles. In the UK we also offer a range of other gift and stationery products illustrated with Frith photographs, although many of these are not available for delivery outside the UK – see our web site for more information on the products available for delivery in your country.

## THE INTERNET

Over 100,000 photographs of Britain can be viewed and purchased on the Frith web site. The web site also includes memories and reminiscences contributed by our customers, who have personal knowledge of localities and of the people and properties depicted in Frith photographs. If you wish to learn more about a specific town or village you may find these reminiscences fascinating to browse. Why not add your own comments if you think they would be of interest to others? See **www.francisfrith.com**

## PLEASE HELP US BRING FRITH'S PHOTOGRAPHS TO LIFE

Our authors do their best to recount the history of the places they write about. They give insights into how particular towns and villages developed, they describe the architecture of streets and buildings, and they discuss the lives of famous people who lived there. But however knowledgeable our authors are, the story they tell is necessarily incomplete.

Frith's photographs are so much more than plain historical documents. They are living proofs of the flow of human life down the generations. They show real people at real moments in history; and each of those people is the son or daughter of someone, the brother or sister, aunt or uncle, grandfather or grandmother of someone else. All of them lived, worked and played in the streets depicted in Frith's photographs.

We would be grateful if you would give us your insights into the places shown in our photographs: the streets and buildings, the shops, businesses and industries. Post your memories of life in those streets on the Frith website: what it was like growing up there, who ran the local shop and what shopping was like years ago; if your workplace is shown tell us about your working day and what the building is used for now. Read other visitors' memories and reconnect with your shared local history and heritage. With your help more and more Frith photographs can be brought to life, and vital memories preserved for posterity, and for the benefit of historians in the future.

Wherever possible, we will try to include some of your comments in future editions of our books. Moreover, if you spot errors in dates, titles or other facts, please let us know, because our archive records are not always completely accurate—they rely on 140 years of human endeavour and hand-compiled records. You can email us using the contact form on the website.

Thank you!

For further information, trade, or author enquiries
please contact us at the address below:

**The Francis Frith Collection, Oakley Business Park,
Wylye Road, Dinton, Wiltshire SP3 5EU England.**
Tel: +44 (0)1722 716 376  Fax: +44 (0)1722 716 881
e-mail: sales@francisfrith.co.uk  **www.francisfrith.com**